Online Business for Spiritual Visionaries

*Sharing Inner Wisdom
as a Successful Entrepreneur*

Other Books in this Series:
Online Business for Spiritual Visionaries

Online Community for Spiritual Visionaries: How to Successfully Gather and Nurture Your Virtual Tribe by Jeff Carreira with Sophie Peirce.

Online Curriculum for Spiritual Visionaries: How to Create Transformative Programs by Jeff Carreira with Sophie Peirce.

Free Resources from Jeff Carreira

Life Without Fear: Meditation as an Antidote to Anxiety with Jeff Carreira. Visit lifewithoutfear.online

Secrets of Profound Meditation: Six Spiritual Insights that will Transform Your Life with Jeff Carreira.
Visit secretsofprofoundmeditation.com

Foundations of a New Paradigm: A 6-part program designed to shift the way you experience everything with Jeff Carreira.
Visit foundationsofanewparadigm.com

Online Business for Spiritual Visionaries

Sharing Inner Wisdom as a Successful Entrepreneur

Jeff Carreira

with Sophie Peirce

EMERGENCE EDUCATION
Philadelphia, Pennsylvania

Copyright © 2021 by Jeff Carreira.

All rights reserved. Except as permitted under U.S. Copyright Act of 1976, no part of this publication may be reproduced, distributed, or transmitted in any form or by any means, or stored in a database or retrieval system, without the prior written permission of the publisher.

ISBN- 978-1-954642-05-8

Emergence Education
P.O. Box 63767
Philadelphia, PA 19147
EmergenceEducation.com

Cover and interior design by Sophie Peirce.

Printed in the United States of America.

Contents

Introduction ix

How to Think about Wealth and Success 1
   My Journey into Spiritual Entrepreneurship 3
   How To Share Your Wisdom While Living in the World 7
   Think about Abundance, Not Accumulation 8

How to Think about Your Business 17
   Starting on the Right Track 18
   The Essential Business Roles 20
      The Visionary Function 21
      The Technical Function 22
      The Management Function 23
   Let Your Business Work for You 26
      Following The 80/20 Rule 26
      1000 True Fans 32
      Better Business 32

How to Nurture and Grow Your Audience 37
The Two Communication Cycles of your Business 38
Communications to Your Community (Your Nurture Cycle) 38
Communications to the Public (Your Promotional Cycle) 41
Content Marketing 48
Selling Content with Content 49
Invite People into a World of Possibility 51

Product Design and Technology 55
Your Mailing List 56
Mailing List Technology: 57
List Building Strategy - The Optin/ Lead Magnet 60
Lead Magnet Examples 61
Lead Magnet Deliverability 62
Lead Magnet Alignment 63
Content Based Business Products 65
Your Ecosystem of Products: Designing a Product Series 65
Product Technology 69
Web Presence: How people can find you. 71
Payment Processor: How people can pay you 75
Delivery Needs for Specific Product Types 76

Some Final Words of Encouragement 81

Thank You and Suggestions for Further Reading 87

Introduction

I FEEL VERY GRATEFUL for the life that I live. I spend my time sharing what I love the most with people who love it, and I earn a living doing it. I wrote this book because I want that for you too.

This book was written specifically for spiritual visionaries or what I call 'Artists of Possibility'. Artists of Possibility are people who have devoted themselves, for years or even decades, to an inner quest for wisdom. They are people who have journeyed out beyond the familiar and have discovered extraordinary possibilities that they want to share with others. If you are reading this book, it probably sounds a lot like you.

I'm not an expert on business, but I have been successful with one online business model that I have developed and refined for almost two decades. It is a business model that creates transformative opportunities in the form of books, courses, programs and retreats and offers them to a growing community of people.

In this book, I am going to share my business model with you, along with everything I've learned that makes it successful. This is not the only way to be successful in business as a spiritual visionary, but it's the one I've been successful with and it's the one I want to share with you. I encourage you to read these pages carefully and think about how you can apply the insight they contain to your own situation and the wisdom you want to share.

I also want to take this opportunity to thank my collaborator, Sophie Peirce. As you will learn in this book, Sophie is my business partner, and although the book was written in my voice, she contributed a great deal of the knowledge being shared.

Thank you, and I wish you all the very best with your visionary business.

Sincerely,

Jeff Carreira

IF YOU TRULY HAVE SOMETHING VALUABLE TO SHARE, *you almost have an obligation* **TO SET UP A SIMPLE BUSINESS** *that will allow you to share it.*

I BELIEVE YOU CAN BUILD A LIFE WHERE YOU WILL BE ABLE TO

do what you love,
with people you love,
for the reasons you love

... AND YOU CAN'T GET WEALTHIER THAN THAT.

How to Think about Wealth and Success

IN THIS FIRST CHAPTER I offer some thoughts about how I have come to think about running a business. It offers an orientation toward business that I've embraced more and more consciously over the years. I believe that the way we orient ourselves toward business from the start, and the way we think about being in business ongoingly, is of paramount importance. Your fundamental attitudes and beliefs about yourself, your potential for success, and what it means to be in business, will determine what is ultimately possible for you.

The ideas you are asked to consider in these first pages, along with the work of aligning your own beliefs and attitudes with them, can open up new worlds of potential for you. This is the most exciting, and most important part of your adventure in entrepreneurship.

I BELIEVE THAT THOSE OF US WHO HAVE DEVOTED OURSELVES TO SPIRITUAL LIFE

HAVE A RESPONSIBILITY TO *live in abundance.*

My Journey into Spiritual Entrepreneurship

I want to tell you a little bit about myself and the journey that led me to owning a business that is based on my spiritual passions. Many years ago, in 1992, I gave up a lucrative career as a research engineer in the telecommunications industry so that I could pursue my heart's deep longing for spiritual practice and awakening. I had always known that there was more to life than earning money and being comfortable, and I finally decided to pursue what I truly thought mattered in life.

For twenty years I lived in an intentional community that was focused on spiritual practice and awakening. During that time I needed to work in order to support myself. Initially I worked as an engineering contractor and later as a school teacher. Both of these occupations allowed me to maximize my income while leaving me time to pursue my spiritual interests.

Eventually, I was offered a job as the marketing and education director within the community that I had become a prominent member of. One of the things I was responsible for was developing and running virtual programs that supported people's spiritual practice and growth.

When I started running virtual programs and a global membership program, I did it without the benefit of the easy access to information and software that the world wide web offers today. The internet existed, and I had used it as an engineer, but it was still limited to professional and mainly technical uses. My first virtual programs were delivered via telephone, using a free telephone conference service.

In 2005, I ran my first fully online program. It was a nine hour event that gathered an impressive group of prominent spiritual luminaries of the time, including Deepak Chopra and Ken Wilber. This was years before others in the spiritual world had thought

ONLY *abundance* **LEADS TO** *abundance.*

IF YOU WANT *abundance* **YOU HAVE TO BE** *abundant* **NOW.**

of doing the kind of online summits that have become popular today. Without knowing what we were doing (no one really did back then) we had 10,000 people register for our first online event.

A few years later the spiritual community that I was a part of disbanded, leaving me without a source of income and with no recognizable work history for fifteen years. I published my first book, *The Miracle of Meditation* in 2012 the same year that the disbanding of the community I was in began. I offered my book for free as an ebook on a website that I had built myself. I researched Facebook advertising and started running an ad for the book. I tweaked the copy of the ad until I was getting about 80 downloads a day.

It was not long before I had collected 2500 email addresses from ebook downloads and I decided that was enough. Since that time Facebook has changed its advertising algorithm numerous times and it is now near impossible to get such good results for the little amount of money I was spending. If I knew then, what I know now, I would have let that ad run until it stopped performing. But as they say, hindsight is 20/20.

By the time I published *The Miracle of Meditation*, I had already offered my first online retreat as a teacher in my own right (That is, outside of the community that I had taught inside of for years already). 100 people registered paying $100 each. I did similar retreats four times over the next couple of years and that was my business model. It didn't earn a lot of money, but I felt wealthy because for me, the measure of wealth has never been dollars. I have always measured wealth as *the ability to do what I love, with the people I love, for the reasons I love*. By that standard I was very wealthy and I still am.

Since those early years my business has grown. I've published 25 more books and have taught numerous online programs using a variety of different structures. Sometimes I've taught on my own and sometimes with teaching partners. I've also led in-person meditation retreats in Denmark, Canada, Australia, Sri Lanka,

Brazil and throughout the United States. I have successfully run two intensive teacher training programs that included both online and in-person components. I have been delighted to see my business expand, but I have to admit that I felt just as wealthy when my business was small, as I do now. That's because the whole time I was able to do *what I love, with the people I love, for the reasons I love.*

If you want to be wealthy in the way I'm describing then this book is for you. In these pages I will show you how to turn what you love into courses and programs that can be offered as part of a business that brings tremendous value to the people it serves. I will also teach you some solid business practices for creating a successful enterprise, by which I mean one that will allow you to create a lifestyle in which you are able to do what you love, with the people you love, for the reasons you love.

I have written this book for spiritual visionaries like yourself. And by that I mean people who have plumbed the deeper realms of the human soul and spirit, and returned with gifts, visions, insights and tools that they now feel compelled to share with anyone who is drawn to them.

As someone who devoted so much of your life to the deeper realms of the human experience, you might find the whole idea of making money from the gifts you have received a bit off putting. I hear you. The gifts of grace that we received from divinity were given with perfect generosity. No matter what it took to get us there, when we finally came upon those gifts they were bestowed upon us, given to us with the same generosity that an apple is given freely from the tree it grows on. The idea of turning around and selling that gift for money can feel wrong.

This is certainly one way of looking at it, and it's valid, but I also want to share another perspective.

We live in a world that often seems to be overwhelmed with ignorance and a lack of awareness of the deeper values and potentials of the human spirit. At the same exact time, so many of us have done profound inner work that has revealed to us depths of insight and understanding that our world desperately needs. It is my belief that one of the greatest untapped human resources in the world today is the wealth of wisdom currently contained in so many spiritual luminaries, like yourself, that has yet to be shared with a wider public. That is why part of my work is to support people like you to be able to successfully share what you have discovered on your journey.

Of course that doesn't necessitate starting a business venture - *and yet* in the western world we live in a culture that necessitates that we generate income somehow.

How To Share Your Wisdom While Living in the World

Generally speaking, there are three ways that a spiritual visionary can live in our world while sharing the wisdom they have to offer.

- Share your wisdom freely and rely on donations to support yourself.
- Find work that maximizes your income and leaves you time to share your wisdom.
- Build a business that will allow you to earn an income by sharing your wisdom.

Relying on donations is a viable option, but securing donations takes as much work, and is as much a business as anything else. If you don't do the work to secure sufficient donations to survive sustainably, you end up living a life of poverty and the struggle to survive in poverty takes up as much of your time and energy as any job would.

When I was working as an engineering consultant I could earn a good deal of income over a few months and then survive for a few more months before needing to find more work. Later as a school teacher, I worked during the school year and had summers off. In both cases I eventually became dissatisfied with the experience of living in two worlds. I wanted to spend all of my time in the world of spiritual pursuit and revelation.

I wrote this book to share practices and attitudes that have been immensely valuable in creating my own online business. I believe that if you follow this advice, you can build a life that will allow you to share what you are most passionate about full time, and earn a decent income doing it. In other words, you will be able to do what you love, with people you love, for the reasons you love - and you can't get wealthier than that.

Before we dive in, I want to highlight that the focus of my business is not to grow as big as possible - rather, it is to be as efficient as possible. I am sure that I could generate a larger income if I spent more time and energy building my business, but I'm not in business to build a bigger business. My business is all about sharing what I'm passionate about, in a way that meets my financial needs.

In this book you are going to find the very best, practical advice on how to build simple business structures and create a reliable source of income without compromising your values.

Think about Abundance, Not Accumulation

I am a mystical philosopher and my business and work practices are a reflection of my beliefs about reality and my philosophy of life. So I'm going to use this part of the chapter to share my deepest understanding about where success and abundance in life truly come from.

I believe that those of us who have devoted ourselves to spiritual life have a responsibility to live in abundance. Why? Because what we've discovered through our spiritual practice is that life is divine and bountiful and generous, and we want our life to be an expression of that.

My own business experience and the work I've done supporting others with their business ventures, has shown me that human beings don't naturally live in abundance because our culture encourages us to live *in pursuit of* abundance. I want to share the secret of living in abundance right here at the start.

Only Abundance Generates Abundance.

The secret recipe for abundance is that abundance leads to abundance. No amount of hard work and struggle will ever lead to abundance. Struggle and hard work lead to more struggle and hard work. Only abundance leads to abundance.

If building your business starts to feel like too much struggle and hard work, take a step back and find the place of abundance in what you are doing right now. Step out of the place where you feel fear and need, and into the place where you recognize what a privilege it is to be able to build a life doing exactly what you love, with people you love, for reasons you love. If you want abundance you have to be abundant now.

Thinking in terms of doing something now to get something later is the essence of lack. Lack is rooted in the idea that something is missing from the here and now, that can only come later. If you are working to build a business so your future will be full and abundant, you are living in lack, and living in lack never leads to abundance. Building the life of your dreams needs to be exactly what you want to be doing, not something you feel you have to do so you can live the life of your dreams later. You have to find a way to love what you are doing now.

LIFE *doesn't become* ABUNDANT

LIFE *already is* ABUNDANT

develop the habit of Being in abundance.

Anything you do now to become abundant later reinforces the experience of lack. There is nothing that you can do now to become abundant later that won't reinforce the exact experience of lack that you're trying to transcend.

To be abundant, you must find a way to be abundant in your life exactly the way it is right now.

If you can't live in abundance in the life you're living right now, you won't be able to find abundance in any other life. Life doesn't *become* abundant because life *already is* abundant. Abundance is not about accumulation. It is an attitude we adopt about life and it doesn't require anything else.

I've worked with people who earn a great deal of money and have more material things than they need, but they are still living in lack. You can live in lack with a lot of money just as easily as you can live in lack with very little money. You can live in lack in any lifestyle. The experience of lack is not rooted in circumstance. It is a habitual way of relating to life as a whole.

To live in abundance you have to break the habit of being in lack and develop a habit of being in abundance. When you're living in abundance you inevitably attract more abundance, because we always get more of what we are already. If you're living in lack and trying to find abundance, you inevitably attract more lack and a stronger need to try harder to find abundance.

I've seen people spend decades thinking they're going to get out of lack by engaging in the next venture or the next lifestyle shift, only to find that the quest for abundance goes on. And just like any habit - the longer it goes on, the harder it is to break.

If you want to live in abundance you need to stop *trying* to live in abundance and discover how to actually be in abundance right now, in the life you're already living. That means being in abundance while doing all the work it will take to build your business. *Key*

You need to find a way to shift into a sense of dramatic abundance and appreciation for the life you are already living. You have

11

Artists of Possibility **ARE PEOPLE WHO HAVE ACCESS TO THE DEEPER, OFTEN HIDDEN ASPECTS OF REALITY** *and feel compelled* **TO SHARE THAT KNOWLEDGE WITH THE WORLD.**

to be thrilled to be in a position to build a business that can support the life of your dreams. You don't build a business to find abundance, you find abundance in building a business.

Of course it's easy to say, "All we need to do is be abundant now." But there's always a big part of us that consciously and unconsciously is going to complain, "You just can't BE abundant. That's just pretending. Something needs to change before you can be abundant."

This kind of thinking keeps us stuck in a perception where we never feel like we've made it. There is always one more thing that needs to change before we can be happy with the life we're living.

The important question to ask yourself is:

Can you move past the belief that abundance isn't possible right now, and instead, know without doubt that abundance is already yours?

If you think abundance is only possible later, abundance will remain out of reach because believing that abundance will come later implies that abundance isn't happening now. There will always be a later. There will always be something else to do.

The point to remember is this: Life is not perfect. You can always look at problems and challenges and conclude that something is wrong. There will always be things that aren't working, but that doesn't make life less abundant. Life is always full. Realizing the fullness that is always the essence of life, is what true abundance is.

My story is a good example of how to shift into abundance because I didn't start out feeling abundant. Like most people, I was insecure and afraid most of the time as a child. It wasn't until I devoted my life to spiritual pursuit that things started changing dramatically for me.

At that point, I didn't care about being abundant. All I wanted to do was meditate and learn about spiritual ideas. I didn't care about money or possessions. I didn't care about any of the things that most people associate with abundance. In fact I quickly accumulated $40,000 of debt. But even with debt I felt rich, because I was doing what I loved, with the people I loved, for the reasons I loved. I was building a habit of true wealth and abundance.

When the life I was living in a spiritual community fell apart, I moved on and constructed the amazing life that I'm living now. I believe that the reason I was able to do that was because for years I was completely devoted to pursuing what I loved most. I wasn't involved in spiritual pursuits for some other reason. It wasn't a means to some other end. It was what I loved. And it is still what I love and still what my life is all about. I am still living my passion.

To live in abundance, we need to live our passion. We've all heard this, but we might not have thought enough about what it would really mean for us to do that.

I remember a book called *Do What You Love and the Money Will Follow*. My experience tells me that there was something they didn't say on the cover. I think the book should have a subtitle that reads, *But Only If You're **Not** Doing It For The Money*; because if you're doing what you love to earn money, you're not really *doing* what you love. You're *using* what you love, and there's a big difference.

If you live your passion, how can life not work out for the best?

When you're living your passion, your entire life starts to align with what you are passionate about. And isn't that what we want? Isn't what you really want, to live a life that you're truly passionate about?

My own life has included years of struggle and mounting debt. I'd get out of debt and go into more debt because every time I made money I used it to pursue more of what I was passionate about. And I didn't really care that I was in debt because I was doing what

I loved. In a mysterious way there was a momentum building during that time that now carries my life abundantly forward.

For any of you that are at a point where you're feeling the challenge and the struggle, I want you to know that I know there are times when the whole thing feels like a big rock that you have to push uphill. And the problem with pushing a rock uphill is that if you're not actively pushing it up then it's rolling back down on you. Pushing uphill requires constant effort. But if you're doing what you love, it won't feel awful, because you're doing what you love.

Eventually you'll start to feel the hill level off. It's not going up anymore. The rock is easier to push. Now you can rest a little if you want. And then you realize that your life is starting to move without you needing to push at all. It starts to move out of your hands. Your abundance and success is happening on its own and you're almost having to run to catch up.

You've realized a life of abundance, but of course your life was already abundant because you were already doing what you loved.

As we go through the remainder of this book please keep this chapter in mind. Even when you are doing the hard work of building your business, you always want to be doing it from inside a life of abundance. You don't want to be thinking of it as something unpleasant that you have to do so you can get what you want later. Instead, think of it as living your dream of building a business that will support you to share your deepest gifts with the world.

How to Think about Your Business

Now that you know a little about me and my business and life philosophy, I want to jump into the nuts and bolts of creating a successful online business. In this chapter I will present the high level roles and functions that you will need to play or fill, to make your business work, and then in later chapters we will get a little more granular in exploring exactly how to set up basic core elements that will ensure your business works for you and you don't end up working for it.

Please don't skip this chapter. It may seem like a mile high view of a business, but keeping track of your business from this elevation is crucial. You don't want to lose sight of the forest for the trees. What we discuss in this chapter is just as important for your success as any ground level task that you will perform.

I want to state again that my work is dedicated to supporting and nurturing the growth of spiritual visionaries, or what I call 'Artists of Possibility'. Artists of Possibility are people who have access to the deeper, often hidden aspects of reality and feel compelled to share that knowledge with the world. In their moments of realization they see potentials that are not manifest yet, and what they see is an indescribably wondrous possibility for the world that they are deeply compelled to bring to life.

One of the ways that I want to support Artists of Possibility is by guiding them to create a business out of their inner vision that will allow them to dedicate their entire lives to sharing it.

As I've already mentioned, I realize that often Artists of Possibility don't love the business of business. I get that. I don't love it either. I love the ideas, perspectives and experiences that I want to share with the world and it is through having a business that I am able to do that. It is because I don't love the business of business that I emphasize efficiency when it comes to building and running your own business venture.

Efficiency in business is attained by taking the necessary time and energy at the start to set up well functioning systems, and keeping those systems as simple as possible. Complexity does not necessarily add value to your business and unnecessary complexity tends to demand more of your energy.

In this chapter you will find a description of the basic business structure that I use and have optimized over nearly a decade. Everything I share with you is what I do and I am confident that most, if not all of it, is fully applicable to your own situation.

STARTING ON THE RIGHT TRACK

There is an ancient Chinese proverb that wisely asserts *If you don't change direction, you'll end up where you're headed.* Unfortunately when it comes to a business, changing direction mid-course is a lot like turning an ocean liner around. Once that big ship has built up momentum going in the wrong direction, it takes a long time and a lot of energy to turn it around. This means that it's a lot easier to set out on the right course in the first place than it is to change course later.

In this section I will state as clearly as possible where I think you should be heading now as you're getting started and how I think you can get there so you won't need to change course later. In brief, you should be heading toward the creation of a business that will work for you and liberate your time and energy so you can spend as much of your life as possible generating and perfecting the content you love and want to share with the world. It is now, at the beginning of your business venture when you can do yourself a huge favor by getting things going in the right direction.

The most valuable book I've found about how to set up your business structure is Michael E. Gerber's *The E-Myth*. I've read it many times and return to it anytime I feel my business practices might have gone astray. The most important thing I learned from Gerber was that a good business is built out of simple and repeatable systems and processes. And my experience is that once the systems and processes are in place, the business of the business almost runs itself.

The basic premise of *The E-Myth* is that people usually start a business because they love their content and/or product and want to share it. Many businesses fail because the people who start them don't actually want to do the work of creating a successful business and give up when they find out what it will take. I wrote this book because I want to show you that creating your own business doesn't have to be an overwhelming challenge. Starting a business and making it successful takes hard work, but if you do it the way I describe, a lot of the work will be exciting and fulfilling, and as you see that your life as an Artist of Possibility is taking shape right before your eyes, it won't seem so painful at all.

In *The E-Myth*, Gerber encourages you to get your business to run like a fast food chain. That might not sound very appealing, but if you think about it, it makes sense. What he means is that you want to put systems in place that make everything work simply and repeatedly, so you don't end up running the business by the seat of your pants.

People who run their business by the seat of their pants almost always work inefficiently. They do one thing and then another, they try something and then something new, then they switch again to something else. They never stick to anything long enough to systematize it or see if it truly works. They end up reinventing the same wheels over and over again and using a variety of different tools to get the same jobs done.

If you systematize your business, and keep the systems simple and efficient, your business will simplify your life, not complexify it. You want the systems of your business to be boring. That means that it contains a few tasks that are easily completed, and can be done over and over again in exactly the same way.

If you're like me, you will start out as a solopreneur, a one-person show, and that means you will be the person driving every system and doing all the tasks. But, if the systems are well defined, you will hardly need to think about what you're doing. When it comes to the business of the business, you want to be able to do the work with your eyes closed. That way you can save your conscious attention and energy for your content creation and the higher level visionary thinking that your business will require to guide it forward. If setting up systems is not something you're good at, find a partner who is, and let them help you. Setting up simple and efficient business systems and processes from the start is going to save you enormous amounts of time and energy later. It's well worth the effort.

THE ESSENTIAL BUSINESS ROLES

When I read *The E-Myth* I learned that there are three essential roles that must be fulfilled in any business. Keeping these roles in mind, even during the years that I was a solopreneur playing all three roles myself, has been very important to me. Keeping these roles clear will allow you to work on all of the essential aspects of running a business without letting any one of them fall through the cracks.

The Three Essential Business Roles

1. The visionary function ✓
2. The technical function ✓
3. The management function ✓

As I said, you may initially play all three roles yourself, but it is still crucial to keep these roles separate in your own mind. If you don't, it is likely that you will shortchange one of them, the one you like the least, and that will negatively impact your whole venture.

The Visionary Function

Someone in the business has to be holding the vision. That is the person who knows, and doesn't forget, <u>what the business is really about.</u>

It's easier than you might think to forget what you're doing, especially when you find yourself responding to the demands of running a business. You end up doing things that don't feel quite right and then when you step back and look, you realize you've been creating content or selling products that are not aligned with why you created your business in the first place. They might be good products, they might even be great, but they're not what you got in business for.

This often happens when lucrative avenues for expansion emerge that are not really part of your original vision and core mission. You stray from your vision and mission with the justification that it will generate income that will support the rest in the future. There certainly may be times in especially favorable circumstances when this is a good strategy, but too often these sidetracks end up dragging your whole enterprise in the wrong direction and it can take immeasurable effort to get back on track.

The visionary is the person who keeps watch over the vision and mission of the business. They are the one who ensures that decisions are aligned with the original intent and they hold primary responsibility for charting the future of the business and navigating through the sea of opportunities that might arise. This is an essential role and if you are playing multiple roles in your business, you need to be disciplined about giving yourself time to be the visionary. You can't do this on the fly. You need to set aside time that is dedicated to contemplating the state of your business and its future.

The Technical Function

The technician is the person who does the work of creating the products that you sell. If you are selling online courses like I do, the technician is the person (or persons) who write the curriculums, plan the sessions, create the materials, build the web pages, and manage participation in the courses and programs.

Of course your business doesn't just create courses and programs, it also markets and publicizes them. The technician also produces the sales and marketing materials - ads, flyers, promotional items, etc. - that you need in order to sell your products. The technicians are the producers, the ones who make stuff. The technical parts of my business revolve around creating courses, programs and marketing materials on the one hand, and maintaining websites and e-commerce systems on the other. I am primarily responsible for the first tasks, and my partner is primarily responsible for the others. We split the role of the technician in our company to match our different skill sets and technical capacities.

The Management Function

The manager is the person who makes sure that all aspects of the business are working harmoniously together. The manager makes sure that content is ready when programs and courses are scheduled to start, and that sales copy is written when it is time to begin promoting a course or sell a product. They make it all work. They keep everyone focused on the most important tasks at each moment.

The visionary is focused on the vision, the technician is focused on production, and the manager is focused on making it all work together.

As an Artist of Possibility you might find yourself being least interested in the management function, but remember, the management function is the heart and soul of the business. Unfortunately, it can sometimes be, and often is, the part we are least interested in. Still, it is an absolutely essential function of a healthy business so it has to get done. If you can't or won't do it yourself, you have to find someone who can and will. And whoever is managing your business needs to do it with a sense of abundance. It can't be something that someone is just trying to get through, they have to love doing it, at least while they're busy with it. There are indeed people who love managing the operations of a business. If you find such a person, reward them well for their valuable contribution so they stay with your business forever. They're worth it.

BUILDING WELL-DEFINED BUSINESS SYSTEMS IS *liberating.*

Case Study: The Essential Roles in My Business

At the time of writing this, my business operates with two full time people, me and my business partner. In terms of roles, I'm the primary visionary, content creator and marketing manager. My partner is the primary technician and manager, taking care of all of our online systems, communications and workflows.

Although we have split the essential roles of the business, we also tend most often to work together. But even though we work together on most things, it is still critically important that we are clear about who holds primary responsibility for what. If we don't know who is responsible for what, things will fall to the floor between us. We don't want to find ourselves in a situation where we are looking at each other saying, "I thought you were doing that."

In addition to the two of us, we hire a few different consultants and contractors to do tasks in areas where we lack the necessary expertise and/or skill.

I love this business model because it is simple and manageable. Having a partner that compliments your skills is an amazing benefit, and you can always find good contractors to do specific tasks through online websites like Fiverr, Upwork and Indeed. I highly recommend that you set up something similar to this structure for your own business.

Let Your Business Work for You

Now that you understand the need for the visionary, technical and management roles in your business, it's time to start outlining the core elements of your business structure. The core structure will form the engine that drives your business. But before we get to that, let me offer a few last thoughts about why the up front energy you spend creating business systems will be well worth it in the long run.

Building well-defined business systems is liberating. When your systems work well you can get everything done quickly and efficiently and that frees up your time to focus more on the aspects of your work that you love the most, which, if you're like me, is creating new and better content. You don't have to be excited about building a business, but you should be excited about putting the structures in place that will free up your time for what you truly love - sharing the content that got you into business in the first place. The better your systems are from the start, the less attention it will take to run them later.

As an Artist of Possibility, unless your particular artistry is business, you probably want the business part of your business to consume as little of your time and energy as possible. The way to achieve this is to invest time in building business structures and systems that work, so that you don't have to keep tinkering with them to make them work later. You want to create a business that works for you, otherwise you will end up working for your business.

Following The 80/20 Rule

You may have heard of the 80/20 rule. It is a valuable way to think, and it guides a great deal of my decision making when it comes to business. The rule states that 20% of your effort generates

20% of your effort → generates 80% of income

80% of your profit, and the remaining 80% of your energy, only generates the remaining 20% of your profit.

So, when it comes to the business side of the business, I want to give 20% of my energy to that which generates 80% of the profit. Then I can devote the other 80% of my energy to developing my artistry and creating the content that I want to share with the world.

This approach has worked well for me and I think it will work well for you too. Essentially, I can devote one day out of a five day work week to the business of the business and the other 4 days to writing books, creating curriculum for new programs, teaching courses online and leading in-person retreats. Since writing books, creating curriculum, teaching courses and leading retreats is what I love to do, I'm living in abundance all the time. And since I know that doing the business of the business is allowing me to do what I love, I end up loving that too.

Think of your business like a merry-go-round. Remember when you were a child and the merry-go-round was full of kids and you had to run hard and fast to get it to start spinning, but then once it got up to speed, you could stand back and keep it going with just an occasional light tap. The merry-go-round's own momentum did most of the work, you just needed to add a little extra push every now and again so that it didn't slow down.

That is how I want you to think about your business. Put in the necessary energy up-front, then allow it to build momentum until you can keep it going with just an occasional light tap. I'm sure that sounds good to you. The thing to keep in mind is this, *you can't rush through building your business*. Invest time and energy into building it well. If you don't, you will end up with something like a broken down car that keeps needing repairs. Remember the guy in your neighborhood with the old car who spent all day with his head under the hood? If you love working on cars that's fine, but if you don't, it may lead to a lot of unnecessary frustration.

Another way that I want you to think about your business is as an engine. Once you have your basic systems in place you want them to function well. That means having things happen in predictable ways, one step after another, resulting in people getting the content they love and paying you for it. When your business systems are in place, you want to see that they are generating income for you, even when you're not looking. You want to be able to send an email out announcing a new program or a new book, and wake up the next morning to see how many have sold while you were asleep. When your business is consistently generating income, you can relax.

Case Study:
The Value of Great Relationships and Well Defined Systems

As the primary visionary in my business, I make sure that every two months or so my partner and I map out our entire business on paper or whiteboard. We make diagrams showing the existing systems that are in place, how they relate to each other, how they are working and where we need improvements. Between my partner and I, we develop three year plans, create curriculum, design courses, write sales pages, set up protected content for participants, plot out marketing sequences and implement sales campaigns. Between us we know who does what, what needs to be done when, when we need to work together, and when it is more efficient to work independently. As a result the turnaround time between content/product idea, to sales and delivery is usually achieved in a very short space of time, and we are able to produce content and products in volumes that far exceeds even our own expectations.

CREATE A BUSINESS *that will work for you* **BY LIBERATING YOUR TIME AND ENERGY TO DO** *more of what you love.*

WHEN YOU'RE LIVING YOUR PASSION,

your entire life starts to align with what you are passionate about.

1000 True Fans

Kevin Kelly, the founder of *Wired* magazine, wrote an essay in 2008 called *1000 True Fans*. The essay offers a valuable perspective for your business. Kelly suggests that all you need to be successful is 1000 true fans. That means 1000 people who love what you do enough to spend $100 over the course of an entire year to keep engaging with you. Having 1000 true fans means that you can generate $100,000 of income. When you think about it this way, it no longer seems like an insurmountable task to earn a full time income doing what you love.

I have taken Kevin Kelly's advice to heart in the creation of my business and what that has translated to for me is giving most of my attention to the people who already love what I do. There is another variation of the 80/20 rule that says that you earn 80% of your profits from 20% of your audience. That 20% is made up of your true fans. They are the ones that love what you do enough to pay you for it. You might be tempted to neglect them because they already love you. Don't do that. Treat your true fans the way they deserve to be treated, like the most important people in the world to your business, because they are.

Yes you will need to continually reach out beyond your existing community to find new people who love what you do, but this is not nearly as important as creating valuable content and experiences for the people who already love you. If you want to be successful, give 80% of your attention to the 20% of your community that is already supporting you.

Better Business

Your business is a series of systems - that means processes that deliver the wisdom you feel compelled to share with the people who want it. You are a spiritual visionary, an Artist of Possibility, a creative mystic. You've discovered something wonderful and profound. You've been blessed with insights and shown a vision of life that has been so transformative for you that all you want to do is share it. You are setting up an online business because that business will allow you to reach dozens, hundreds or even thousands of people who are looking for the same transformative experience that you've had. Sharing your inner wisdom is the foundation of a truly fulfilling life.

As I've said a few times already, you're probably not someone who naturally gravitates toward the business of business. In fact, business might even be a tainted subject for you. As a spiritual visionary, you're likely to be a reluctant entrepreneur. I want to change your mind about business, so you can see how a simple, well thought through, online enterprise can be the foundation upon which thousands of people can benefit from what you have to offer. If you truly have something valuable to share, you almost have an obligation to set up a simple business that will allow you to share it.

When we think of a business we might think of an office full of people wearing suits working to make money, or a factory of conveyor belts building manufactured goods using underpaid labor. Please remove any images of this sort from your mind. My business consists of me living in Philadelphia in the United States and my partner living in Sydney, Australia, thinking about our community and what books, courses, programs, or retreats will best serve it. Then we create the content that we think is most in service to the community and we offer some at a cost and others for free.

The result of our business is that thousands of people gain insight and understanding that brings them step by step closer to living a truly awakened life within a community of other like-minded people. As a byproduct, my business partner and I earn enough income to keep doing what we love the most and part of that is writing and publishing this book so you have the opportunity to create your own business. The kind of business we're talking about, your business, is not an office, a factory, or a store. It's a set of systems that turn ideas into products that can be shared with the people who want to learn from them and can be shared via the internet all over the world.

So now it is time to set up your business.

TREAT YOUR TRUE FANS *like the most important people in the world* **TO YOUR BUSINESS,** *because they are.*

How to Nurture and Grow Your Audience

In your business you take the wisdom you have to share and use it to create products that your audience can use. Your business is essentially educational, and education is essentially communication. What drives your businesses success is constant communication that both nurtures and grows your audience. Your primary responsibility is to communicate constantly with your existing community and with people who might want to join your community.

Please hear that. Your primary responsibility is to communicate constantly with your existing community and with people who might want to join your community. That is what you must do.

With this in mind let me now offer yet another metaphor for your business. Your business is an engine, let's use an infinity symbol to stand for the two communication cycles that are constantly revolving. These two cycles are your business. One of the cycles is your nurture cycle in which you develop and feed your existing audience. The other is your promotional cycle in which you continuously share the value that you have to offer with people who have not heard about you yet.

These two cycles must spin continuously if your business is going to keep going.

The Two Communication Cycles of your Business

Communications to Your Community (Your Nurture Cycle)

The core income generating engine of your business is your communications to your existing mailing list or followers. I like to refer to these people as your community. By joining your mailing list they have already told you that they love what you do. Now it's up to you to nurture the relationship by supporting the growth and development of your community. You do this by sending your community valuable and inspiring content and occasionally making an offer for a larger opportunity that can be purchased by those who want to work more deeply with you. Your ongoing communications with your community can include essays, blog posts, quotes, videos, audio recordings, podcasts, newsletters, and a variety of free online events. Over time a thoughtful communication strategy that is well executed will lead to consistent and reliable income generation from the products you offer.

Once people have joined your mailing list they are part of your community and you have the chance to educate them further about what you do and why it might be valuable for them to pursue it further. You do this by regularly offering your mailing list valuable information and opportunities that are free of charge. We have all experienced what is called list fatigue. That happens when you join a mailing list and receive so many emails that you get sick and tired of getting them and you unsubscribe. You should be wary of creating list fatigue with our community, but you don't do that by not emailing them. You do it by emailing things that are so valuable that they love receiving what you send. That is the key to your success. Every communication you send to your community should offer real and immediate value. Even a sales letter that offers an opportunity to purchase should include wisdom and insights that are valuable even if the person who receives it never purchases the product being offered.

Key

You need to communicate regularly with your audience and you need to do it in a way that makes them love hearing from you every time.

Share:
blog posts
quotes
videos
Audio recordings
podcasts
newsletters
Free online events

[Sales letters that offer value whether they buy or * not *]

products you offer + offers = consistent + reliable income

Figure 1: The Nurture Cycle

Your Nurture Communications

Your Business

YOUR COMMUNITY

Product Sales

Communications to the Public
(Your Promotional Cycle)

The other cycle that your business runs on is made up of the communications that promote what you do to the general public and invite them to become part of your community. This is how you maintain the size of your business, or grow it if you want to. Your promotional cycle will offer small tastes of your content through a variety of outlets that link back to your site where you have a free promotional offer that anyone can receive just by providing their email and signing on to your mailing list. In your promotional communications you will do things like post on social media platforms, write guest blogs and give interviews. On your website your free promotional offer will be something like an eBook, a digital course or a newsletter.

As your promotional communications go out they will attract people who are interested in what you do. Those people will join your mailing list as long as you offer them a good incentive to do so. What you offer people as an incentive to join your mailing list is called a 'lead magnet'. A lead magnet is a free offer, for example, an ebook, an audio recording, a coaching session, a digital download course, or anything else that would be of true value to anyone who would love what you do. Anyone who provides their email address to join your mailing list receives your free gift. Over the years, I've used many different things as lead magnets, and currently I'm using free elearning courses, an ebook and an audio recording of a seminar.

lead magnet
something of true value...

Figure 2: The Promotions Cycle

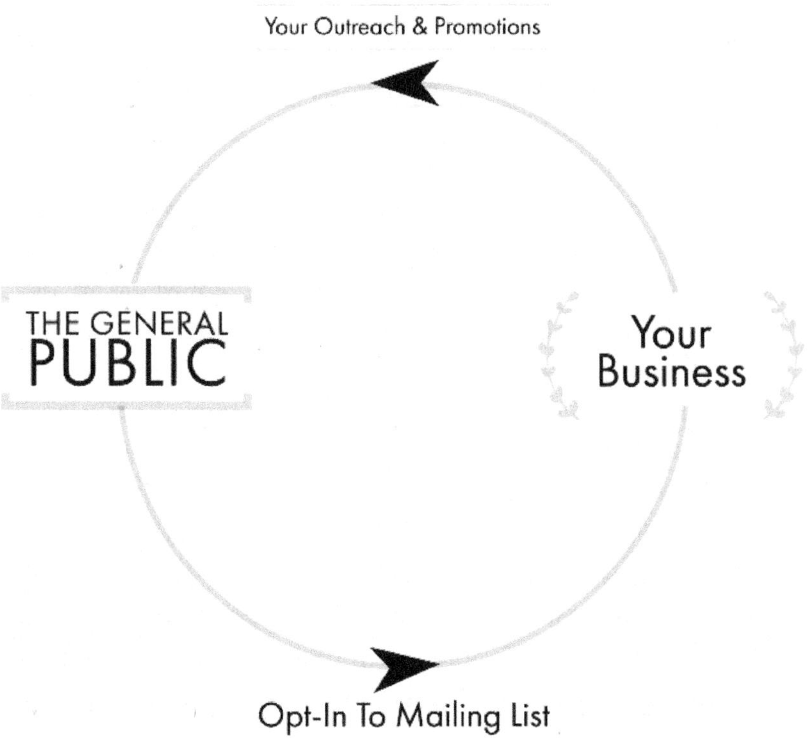

Your Outreach & Promotions

THE GENERAL PUBLIC

Your Business

Opt-In To Mailing List

Your promotional cycle includes all of the communication that you send to people who are not already part of your community, ie. on your mailing list, but might want to be. This needs to be an ongoing part of your business. There are a number of ways that you can communicate with people beyond your current audience and we will review a few of them here.

Social Media Platforms

Facebook, YouTube, Instagram and other social media platforms give you access to huge potential audiences of people. By posting valuable content on them you can attract attention that invites people to get to know you better by joining your mailing list. Keep in mind that in order to benefit from social media promotions you need to post consistently, engage in strategic social activity (liking, commenting, sharing posts etc) and you will most likely need to buy advertising. There are many knowledgeable consultants and books that you can find easily online to help you navigate through the world of social media.

Online Summits, Blog and Podcast Guest Appearances

There are many online summits that you might become a guest speaker on. These will allow you to expose yourself and your ideas to a new audience. You can also write guest posts for popular blogs or be interviewed on podcasts.

Writing and Publishing Books, Podcasts and Hosting Online Summits

Besides being a guest on other people's media outlets you can also create your own. Your website should include an active blog, and you can either create a podcast from your website, or via one of many podcasting platforms. You can also publish books or ebooks that you make available through your own site or on other online marketplaces. I love to write and besides being a way for me to share ideas with people my books serve the added function of acting as promotions for the rest of my work.

Your engine depends on two cycles of communication that are constantly spinning, your nurture cycle and your promotional cycle. Your nurture cycle is where you develop and grow the interest of your existing community and ultimately make sales of the products you create. Your promotional cycle is where you reach out beyond your existing community to introduce people to what you do and invite them to join your community. In the most simple

YOUR PRIMARY RESPONSIBILITY IS TO COMMUNICATE CONSTANTLY WITH *your existing community* **AND WITH PEOPLE** *who might want to join it* terms your business works by reaching out into the world, letting people know what you do, and inviting them to join your mailing list. After that the nurture cycle continually communicates with your mailing list, sharing valuable content with occasional offers for products that can be purchased by those that want them. Keeping these two communications cycles moving is the key to building your business. Imagining your business like an infinity loop with these two communications cycles constantly spinning and meeting in the center. That center point is where your business is. Running your business means keeping these two communication cycles spinning.

Figure 3: The Two Communications Cycles

Your Outreach & Promotions   Your Nurture Communications

THE GENERAL PUBLIC   Your Business   YOUR COMMUNITY

Opt-In To Mailing List   Product Sales

IF YOU ALWAYS GIVE PEOPLE MORE VALUE THAN YOU INTEND TO COLLECT BACK,

you will never have trouble being successful.

Content Marketing

There are many different ways to design your communications cycles and knowing exactly what to mail when, can be tricky. Years ago I discovered a marketing philosophy called content marketing and I never looked back. I am a true believer in this way of marketing because it has worked well for me for many years.

In my experience, I have seen that there are two main things that stop spiritually-minded entrepreneurs from being successful. One is that they don't think they know how to run a business and so don't even try. The second is that they are uncomfortable with promoting themselves and conclude they don't like sales and marketing, so don't give themselves the time they need to be successful. The common factor is that they don't give them a go - they give up.

I once heard an interesting fact on a business podcast. The host boldly announced that there was one attribute that every failed business person had in common and that every successful business person did not share. I was intrigued. The common attribute shared by all failed business people was that they gave up. The common attribute shared by all successful business people was that they didn't give up. Yes you will make mistakes, you will have failures, but if you keep going you will learn and you will improve and eventually you will be successful. If you don't give up, success is guaranteed. And remember, if you are doing what you love, with people you love, for reasons you love, you will be living with a feeling of abundance the whole time anyway.

That being said I can understand how you might not feel comfortable with sales, marketing and promotion. I felt the same way before I discovered content marketing, and now I don't even think of myself as doing sales and marketing anymore. I think of my promotional efforts as an extension of my teaching and educating, which is what I love to do. Even the work of sales, marketing and promotions has become a source of abundance for me.

Selling Content with Content

The basic idea of content marketing is that you sell content with content. Rarely does one like being sold to. No one enjoys receiving an email that says nothing more than, "Hey this product is great - you should buy it". There is very little inherent value in a sales letter like that. The idea with content marketing is that you send people valuable content all the time, even in your promotional materials. That means content that they will love. And as they enjoy and learn from the content you send, they will appreciate you and what you do more and more. They will see how valuable your content is to them and sooner or later they will want to engage more deeply with your work.

I send out short essays once or twice a month to my whole mailing list. I don't write essays like movie trailers that just show you previews of what you will see in the movie. I write them to be complete and valuable in and of themselves. I want people to read my essay and write back to me saying, "Wow, that was really valuable. Thank you for sending that." I don't want there to be anything missing. I want that essay to offer a complete and valuable idea. The essay is only a thousand or maybe two thousand words long, so it can't contain everything, but I want to pack as much value as I possibly can into those words. There are people on my mailing list that will never buy anything from me, but they will benefit for years just from reading my essays - and I am perfectly happy with that.

In addition to essays, I also offer free 90-minute live online workshops and seminars to my entire mailing list about once every six weeks. Sometimes these are associated with a product launch, sometimes they aren't, but they are always complete and valuable in and of themselves. I am constantly hearing back from people who tell me how valuable these seminars are. Many of them will never buy anything from me, and that is fine. I am not in business just to

CONTENT MARKETING WORKS BY *showering people with value.*

THAT'S YOUR MARKETING STRATEGY.

sell. I am in business to share the ideas that inspire me. So sending out free essays is still doing what I love.

I once heard a marketing guru say that if you always give people more value than you intend to collect back, you will never have trouble being successful. "Overwhelm them with value!" They urged. I have run my business according to that principle ever since and I have never regretted it. If you keep giving free valuable content to your community, their appreciation and understanding of what you are offering will grow and many of them over time will purchase from you.

Invite People into a World of Possibility

One of the great examples of content marketing success is the universe of Marvel Comics. Marvel sells comic books and movies and they are experts at content marketing because every comic book they sell and every movie they create is content that advertises other comic books and other movies. Their comic books and movies are all teaching you about the fictional world and the people in it. Each product is a doorway, an invitation, into that world.

From a business perspective, every product Marvel makes is a marketing vehicle for its other products. One Avengers movie will have subplots that carry over from an Ironman movie and that subplot will be continued in a Spiderman movie. What I love about this example is seeing how Marvel is not just selling you products, they are inviting you into their world. As a kid (and even as an adult) I loved that world. I loved learning about the people, places and events of that world, and I also wanted to find out more.

I relate to the example of Marvel Comics because I feel that I am inviting people into a world. The world that I am inviting them into is not a fictional world of superheroes; it is a world of ideas and perspectives and practices that lead to spiritual awakening and enlightenment. I want them to explore the whole world that I have been exploring for decades. My books, programs and retreats offer different avenues for that exploration. Each opportunity that I offer is an invitation - a doorway - into a whole world of discovery that I want to share.

I suggest that you think about what it is that you want to share, and see if you can recognize the world of possibility that you are inviting people into. Spend some time mapping out the different parts of the world that inspire you and think about ways that you can invite people into it. If you design your products carefully each one of them will act as an invitation into the whole world you want to share.

I have devoted my life to exploring the world of mystical philosophy, meditation and spiritual awakening. It is a world that I love and all I want to do is share that world and live inside it with other people who love it. It is not a single book or course that I want to sell. I want to give people access to a world of ongoing discovery. What is the world of discovery that you are inviting people into?

Every social media post, every email, every free online seminar you offer is an invitation to join you in a world of possibility. You create the most compelling invitation when you give the most value that you can in everything that you do. Every essay that I write contains as much value as I can possibly share in it. Even if someone reads just one of my essays and never does anything else with me, I want them to feel that they received tremendous value.

Content marketing works by showering people with value. That's your marketing strategy. You consistently give people valuable things and their appreciation, understanding and trust in you and what you offer grows. Over time people will have received so much value from you that they naturally want to engage with you more deeply through some of your paid products and offerings.

To review - the goal of your promotional cycle is to grow your mailing list; the goal of your nurture cycle is to provide real value to your mailing list and identify those 1000 true fans who will support you to continue doing what you love because they love it too.

Now it is time to share some of the real nuts and bolts of what you will need to design a series of products and offerings that invite people into your world and guide them more deeply into it as far as they want to go.

Product Design and Technology

SO FAR WE HAVE talked about the philosophy of true wealth and abundance and the roles and systems that you need in place to get your business going. We have also discussed the two communication cycles that will drive your business forward and the orientation of content marketing as a framework for communicating with your community. Now we need to talk about how all this is actually done. There is know-how involved in creating a business.

This chapter is more technical than the others in the book. I will make specific recommendations of ways of doing business and resources that you will need. Keep in mind as you read this that I am only sharing the way I do things, and what has worked for me. There are many different ways to set up an online business and I haven't done an exhaustive survey of them all. What I recommend here works for me and I imagine it will work for you, but you may want to research different options to create the systems that will work best for you.

First of all let's start with an obvious fact, an online business exists… well… online. That means it consists of a series of interconnected websites and internet based services that work together. In this chapter we will discuss how to design a series of products that creates the most powerful invitation into the world you want to share. We will also share specific technological tools and services that you will need to utilize in order to build your business effectively, grow your audience and sell your products.

Your Mailing List

We are starting with the most important aspect of your business. Your maikling list is your business. If someday for some reason you were wanting to sell your business the one thing that you would have that would be of value to a potential buyer would be your mailing list. You have done the hard work of identifying people who love what you love and that list is truly valuable. I have been building my mailing list for many years. That list is the most important single aspect of my business. If I were to lose it, I would have to start all over again.

Your mailing list, and the people on it, is your business. Those are the people that love what you love, and some of them love it enough to support you to continue offering it. Building, nurturing, and supporting the people who have joined your mailing list should be your highest priority. Building your mailing list and communicating with it is your most important job.

If you are just starting out you might think that you don't have a mailing list yet, so the first thing that I want to tell you is that you do. Even if you don't think you have one you do. You have friends, family and colleagues who might be interested in what you are doing. You can start with them. Once those contacts are collected somewhere you are going to send an email to them and tell them about the venture that you are starting and invite them to sign on to your mailing list. Those that sign on will stay on your list, those that don't you will delete from the list assuming they don't want more information from you. That is the mailing list you already have. That is the list that you will build on for the rest of the life of your business.

Mailing List Technology:

Your website and social media platforms provide your web presence. That is where people can go to find you and what you do, but that is not where your community is located. So where is your community, ie. your mailing list, located? The heart and soul of your business is the people who are interested in you and what you do, that means, your community, and if you're running an online business that means your mailing list.

Your mailing list is the list of all the people who have told you in one way or another that they care about what you do. That list should contain at least their names and email addresses in it, along with any other information people give you. This list needs to live somewhere and it needs to be somewhere safe. You don't want this to be on your cell phone or your laptop. You want this to be with an email provider that will safeguard your list and allow you to reach out and mail to everyone easily and regularly. You are going to want to keep your list on MailChimp, ActiveCampaign, Aweber, or any of the other mailing platforms available. MailChimp is a very popular option and until your business grows you can use it for free. That is where I started out, and if you don't have a mailing platform already, I recommend that you start there too.

Once you choose a platform you will upload your contacts to create your list. Going forward you can continue to add contacts manually, but it is much easier and more efficient to embed contact forms from your mailing platform into your website, so the process is automated. The contact for will have a space for people to insert

YOUR MAILING LIST, *and the people on it,* IS YOUR BUSINESS.

BUILDING YOUR MAILING LIST AND COMMUNICATING WITH IT *is your most important job.*

YOUR LIST SHOULD BE *cherished* **AND** *safeguarded.*

THE PEOPLE ON IT SHOULD BE *honored, respected and catered to.*

their name and email address and will include a few words inviting them to join your mailing list and offering them something for doing so. Depending on what platform you use, and how you set up your forms, you will be able to track where people came from and segment your list into different groups based on different criteria. This information will be very valuable to you when you start thinking about what you want to mail to who. If you have good tracking information, you wont need to send every email campaign to your entire list all the time. Instead you can target your communications to best reach those people who are most likely to be interested in them.

Let's say that 100 people on your list signed up because they are interested in your books, and you have segmented them into a group called 'Books'. Now, you can send them campaigns only about books and not about retreats. This kind of targeted email strategy is important so that you don't burn your list out. You don't want people getting tired of hearing from you. You can minimise list burnout by only sending information about things you know people are interested in.

Over time you will collect hundreds, thousands, tens of thousands, maybe hundreds of thousands of email addresses. These addresses are the foundation of your business. Your list should be cherished and safeguarded. The people on it should be honored, respected and catered to. Without them you don't have a business. Never forget this. A community based business is a people based business.

List Building Strategy - The Optin/ Lead Magnet

The key to your success will be your ability to nurture and grow your mailing list and now we want to focus on how you grow that list. How do you continually invite people to join your mailing list and provide you with their name and email address? You can very simply have a "join my mailing list" form displayed on your website, but this will probably not be the most effective way to do it. If you want to increase the response you get to your contact form you will want to offer people something of value in exchange for joining. As previously mentioned that offering is what is commonly known as a 'lead magnet'. I've used a number of lead magnets in my business, but those that have worked best have been workshop audio recordings, ebooks, and short digital courses.

Lead Magnet Examples

Workshop Recordings:

I gave a live workshop called *Meditation as an Antidote to Anxiety* and recorded it. (In fact, I record almost everything I teach because recordings of live events can often be used in various ways within your business.) I use that 90-minute audio recording as a lead magnet. That means I have an offer (using a form) on my website that sends them the workshop recording in exchange for their name and email.

ebooks:

Since I love to write, ebooks are a favorite lead magnet of mine. The offer is simple and compelling, I'll send you an ebook in exchange for your name and email address - and by proxy you've joined my mailing list.

Short Virtual Courses:

These are courses that are primarily contained in emails or short videos and accessed through pages on my website. These short virtual courses have worked very well for me as lead magnets. When someone opts-in to one of these free courses, they are added to my mailing list. The course lessons are then delivered via a series of emails that sometimes link to a video and often include questions to contemplate. I receive many emails from people explaining how valuable they find my free courses.

Workshop recordings, ebooks, and courses are the lead magnets that have worked well for me, but there are many other things that you can use.

The best lead magnets will consist of something that can be delivered through email, because once you set that system up it will work for you indefinitely. A mailing platform like MailChimp will allow you to create opt-in contact forms that you can put on your website. On the form you ask people to provide their name and email address to receive your free offer. Once someone provides their name and email address they are added to your mailing list automatically and an email called an auto-responder goes out to them right away. On that email you can thank them for their interest and include the link to whatever offer they signed up to receive. If your offer is a course the mailing platform can send a series of emails spaced every day or two apart. Each email contains the next lesson. Once your list building offer is set up it will keep running indefinitely.

The two things to consider when designing your offers are deliverability and alignment. The third thing to consider - value - goes without saying.

Lead Magnet Deliverability

The consideration of deliverability has to do with how easy it will be to deliver what you offer. The three examples that I mentioned above are all easy to deliver by email. But if you were to offer some physical object like a paperback book, you would need to factor in the time and cost of shipping. Depending on your business, a physical product may be the perfect choice, but you need to consider what it will take to deliver. Another offer that some people make is a free coaching session. There are considerations with that kind of offer that I learned about the hard way.

Lead Magnet Alignment

The consideration of alignment has to do with how well aligned your lead magnet is with the products you ultimately want to sell. If I am giving away ebooks, but I ultimately want to sell a course, that may not be the best match, unless the content of the ebook leads people toward taking the course. To give another example of misalignment, if my lead magnet is a short course about overcoming anxiety but I ultimately want to sell a course on mysticism, that might not be the best match either. So when thinking about your lead magnet you will need to think about creating a strong match between what you are offering for free and what you ultimately want to sell.

lead magnet ≈> what you ultimately want to sell.

Case Study: Appropriate Lead Magnet Design

I offered free 30-minute coaching sessions for one business that I ran. Once I let people know about the offer I got about 30 requests fairly quickly. Given my busy schedule, I soon realized that this was probably not the best free offer for me to have made. It took weeks to schedule all of the free coaching calls and doing all those calls was not the best use of my time at that busy moment in my business. Imagine if I had received 100 requests. No matter what you are offering to build your mailing list you need to think about what it will take to deliver it.

Content Based Business Products

Your Ecosystem of Products: Designing a Product Series

Now you have people on your mailing list and it's time to offer them in-depth opportunities to engage with you and your content that they can pay for. You will need to take the content that you want to share and fashion it into products that people will benefit from. As you design products you will want to think in terms of creating a series of offerings that starts with easy-entry products that are less expensive and don't require too much effort and time to make use of. Then you can create and offer progressively more expensive products that ask more of the customer, and which of course give more value in return. Your product series is itself a form of education. You are teaching people about the world of possibility that you want to share with them and giving them steps that they can follow to travel more and more deeply into it. Below you will find a description of some of the products that I have created and successfully offered.

Digital Download Audio/Video Programs

These programs are created from audio and video content that is offered through a succession of emails that link back to content contained on webpages. Over time I have come to use password protected online course portals to hold the content. My partner built that system for our business, but you can do the same thing using an online education platform like Teachable.com. Generally speaking each lesson of one of my courses includes some written exploration, an audio recording and/or a short video. When someone registers for the course the lessons are delivered in sequence usually spaced a day or two apart.

Live Online Programs

These programs take place via a video conferencing service. I use Zoom Video Conferencing. I have done short courses consisting of just three 60-minute sessions offered once a week. I have also offered longer programs that meet for seven, nine or twelve weeks. Sometimes with longer programs I add one or more daylong retreats (see below) as well. Each program has a password protected online portal containing all the information that registrants need to participate, and there is an email series that welcomes them to the program, tells them how to access the course portal, and reminds them an hour or two before each live session begins with joining instructions.

Live Online Retreats

Retreats have been an important part of my business and I offer them both online and in-person. The structure of my online retreats include full days of engagement via video conferencing for generally between six and as many as eight hours. I have led retreats that take place over one, two or seven days in this format online. Another variation of a retreat format that I have used is to offer only one 60-minute live video session per day for as many as thirty days and the rest of the time people practice and contemplate on their own.

Live Online and In Person Trainings

I have also taught longer training programs that last eight to fourteen months. These trainings are designed with regular live online workshops that are two to three hours in length. These trainings usually offer occasional daylong online retreats and sometimes longer retreats that can be held either online or in-person. These training programs are the most expensive programs that I offer and they afford the most in-depth opportunity for working with me. I generally limit attendance to between twelve to sixteen people.

Ongoing Membership Program

I also run an ongoing membership program. This means that people pay either a monthly or annual fee to be part of an online community that I engage with regularly. Within my membership program I lead retreats and teach courses that are only available to members. Members also get significant discounts on most of the courses and retreats that I offer publicly. I find my membership program to be highly rewarding because it is where I find the people that most love what I do. These are my true fans, the most important people in my universe and I can give them the best of what I have to offer in an ongoing program designed specifically for them.

In addition to these courses, I write and sell books. In my business model the books that I write introduce people to my work and in this way they function more as promotions and invitations than income generators. When I look at who does my courses and retreats they are often people who started working with me by reading one of my books. The books I write also serve another purpose. They are an important part of the ongoing educational opportunity that I offer to my entire community. I write books that I think will support people to move further along on their journey of transformation and spiritual awakening.

YOU ARE NOT JUST SELLING PRODUCTS, YOU ARE *inviting people into a new world.*

Product Technology

As a spiritual visionary entrepreneur you are essentially starting a publishing company. You may not be publishing books, but you are almost certainly publishing something. Blog posts, podcasts, videos, courses, programs, workshops and retreats are all published in the sense that they all offer content in forms that can be used.

If you are publishing books, you need to have systems in place that allow you to write, edit, proof, design, and produce books for sale. If you are publishing online courses, you need systems that allow you to create the curriculum, design the course sessions and deliver them online. If you are publishing retreats you need systems that allow you to find retreat venues, cater to participant's travel needs, and create an optimal retreat experience during the event.

A system is simply a set of actionable steps. One of the reasons my business works well is because I have good systems or sets of actionable steps in place for everything that I offer. That means that everything that needs to be done is outlined in a series of steps and the person responsible for each step knows how to accomplish it. I know how to write books, I know how to hire an editor and proofreader. My design contractor knows how to create aesthetically pleasing covers, my business partner knows how to proofread, and design both paperback and epub format interiors. I've published 26 books to date and each time the process runs through the same basic steps largely without drama. Without doubt we have refined the steps over time as we have learned new skills and techniques, but the overall process of creating a book stays largely the same, and that is the way I want it to be. Reliable, repeatable systems that can be utilized over and over again without demanding too much attention so my attention can go to what I am writing.

The same logic applies to a course or retreat. There are steps involved in planning curriculum, designing lessons, creating an online portal, setting up payments, writing the emails that guide

JEFF CARREIRA

YOU ARE TEACHING PEOPLE ABOUT *the world of possibility that you want to share with them* **AND GIVING THEM STEPS TO TRAVEL MORE AND MORE DEEPLY INTO IT.**

people through the course, setting up the virtual space to hold the sessions, etc. The steps I follow in creating courses are well defined, reliable and repeatable. Each time I run a new course I go through the same steps and I keep those steps simple. That leaves most of my energy and attention free to focus on what I want to teach and share.

Web Presence: How people can find you.

You are ready to create life-transforming products and all you need to know is what you need to produce them, and what you need to deliver them into the lives of the people who want them. If we use an example that we are all familiar with, we can think about a physical store. Your content is the product on the shelf, but you can't just have a product, you need to have a store to display them in. You need a place where people can find your product and purchase it. Or if you think about a mail-order business you need a catalogue that people can order from.

One of the first things you are going to need to get your business started is the online equivalent of your store or catalogue. Generally that means a website or for some, a social media account. Most people will tell you that your business should have its own website, and I agree. In fact I now have five websites, and together they form the majority of my business' web presence. But there are also people who run successful online businesses on social media platforms like Instagram, Facebook or YouTube.

There are a wide variety of options for setting up a website, and the options seem to expand everyday. Carefully thinking through your business needs, your own preferences and skills, and doing some solid research will give you a decent idea of what solution or mix of solutions will work best for you.

I will just outline a few of the options that I use, or have used, and why.

When I built my first website the now popular platform Wordpress didn't exist yet. Instead, I used something called Drupal. When Wordpress became available they offered a much simpler way for me to build and maintain my website. I still use Wordpress and I still find it the best option for me. But today there are other website platforms like SquareSpace that in some ways, make building and maintaining your website even easier. The reason that I, and others, recommend maintaining your own website is because then you are in complete control of how it looks, what content it houses and how it operates. You can create it the way you want it, to serve your needs. Your needs might be perfectly served by Instagram or YouTube, but chances are that at some point you will want something that you just can't do on those platforms.

There are other options for your online presence as well. If you sell physical products there are online marketplaces like Etsy or Society6 where you can display your creations and sell them within a larger umbrella e-commerce solution. If your content is offered in the form of events you can use sites like Eventbrite or Brown Paper Tickets to offer them. And for delivering online programs and courses you can use an all-in-one online education platform like Thinkific or Teachable. If you are less tech savvy, and don't want to do much of the technical work yourself, these newer educational platforms offer a particularly useful alternative to building your own website because they take care of all the maintenance and back end and come loaded with potentially useful features.

The advantage to using a social media platform is that there are millions of people already active on them and with targeted marketing and strategic social activity there is solid potential for bringing new people into your community. I use social media in limited ways for promotion, but my websites are the place that I am always directing people to. I suggest that even if you use social media you maintain your own website. If you enjoy the work of creating a website, with a little bit of skill building there are easy ways to do so. If technical tasks are not your strength you can hire someone to do it for you. Looking within your existing community for help is always a good place to start.

The limitation of global marketplaces, all-in-one platforms, and social media sites is that to use them you have to give up some control. You have to display your content within the parameters that they offer. You might gain access to millions of people who use those platforms, but you don't have control over how you access those people. Social media sites are always changing the ways you can access people and they do it for their advantage not necessarily yours.

I recommend that you set up a website and maintain your own mailing list. Keep it simple. Build it with Wordpress or Squarespace. Use social media to build a following, use a ticket platform to sell admission to events, use an education platform to deliver online programs. But maintain a website that is yours and a mailing list that is independent from all of the other services and platforms that you use. This way you get to have your cake and eat it too. You have the control and the security of your own website and mailing list and you can still take advantage of other online utilities.

Case Study: Limitations of Online Platforms

I once had built a following on a social media platform called Zaads.com. My blog had a thousand followers and then one day they wrote saying that they were closing the website. I had a month to download all my content and there was no way to keep in touch with my followers except to ask them to sign up on my website, very few did. It was early in my business career when that happened and so it wasn't a devastating loss for me, but If I had had 50,000 followers and a business based there it would have been.

Payment Processor: How people can pay you

Now you have your web presence, and your mailing list taken care of. You have great products that you can deliver successfully. You are regularly communicating with your community and letting everyone know what you have to offer. But how do they pay for a product if you have one for sale? You need a simple and safe way for people to pay you online. In short, you need a payment processor and/or an ecommerce solution. There are numerous solutions to the problem of accepting payment online. I started out with something called 1shoppingcart. It is still in use and might be a good solution for you, but currently I use a combination of Shopify and wordpress plugins. Any ecommerce solution you use will cost you something. Shopify charges 2.9% per transaction plus a monthly fee. I find their costs well worth it. I also know a number of people who use Wordpress with a plug-in called WooCommerce, and that seems to work well for them.

I use Shopify for selling books and other physical products as well as in-person retreat registrations. I use a plugin called MemberPress on my Wordpress site for my membership program and for other online courses. MemberPress is technically a membership plugin, but it works great for anything that requires protected content, meaning courses too. For instance, when people register for my courses, they become paid participants and they gain access to the course materials. This has proven to be a valuable solution for me because I run so many courses and by using MemberPress people can gain access to the course materials for all the courses they register for and have access to those materials for life. If you have a Wordpress website, this might also be a good solution for you too. Memberpress (like many other membership plugins) allows me to do what companies like Teachable and Thinkific do. Those platforms weren't around when I started and at this place I am very happy with the systems I have in place, but if you are just starting out I suggest taking a look at some of the all-in-one education platforms that exist to see if one is right for you.

Once you have created reliable systems using some of the technologies we have just discussed, you can present your content online, communicate with your mailing list, and accept payment for purchases. The only thing left is actually delivering the content that someone has paid for. How you deliver the content will depend on what kind of product the content has been packaged into. The last thing we will do is review the basic types of products that you might offer and explore how they can be delivered.

Delivery Needs for Specific Product Types

Books or other physical products

To deliver physical products such as books you will need to use an ecommerce solution like Shopify that allows you to make a sale online and easily pay for, and print shipping labels. Alternatively you can use an online marketplace that includes a store already. Etsy is one such option. Essentially when you use a service like Etsy you sell your content on their store. You have to pay them for the use of their store, but you don't have to set up your own.

Ebooks, Audio Recordings, or Other Digital Products

To deliver digital products you will need to be able to send an email with a link that connects to where the product can be accessed or downloaded. Usually that will mean a page on your website that has a way to download the product. The product will need to be stored somewhere online. I currently use Amazon Web Service (AWS) as cloud storage and it works very well. It is inexpensive and very reliable. If you have a small number of products you can probably upload them directly to the backend of your website, but overtime, numerous large media files can begin to slow down the speed at which your website loads and runs.

Live Online Courses

If you run live online courses you may choose to deliver those through a video conference service like Zoom, so you will need a Zoom account. Zoom is a very popular video conferencing platform, but there are also others. Once you have an account you can set up a repeating meeting that people can access using a web link. Then all you need to do is send them an email thanking them for joining the course and telling them when to click on the link to join each session. I usually also have reminders set to go out to everyone an hour or so before each session starts, reminding them to join and ensuring that they have the joining information at hand. As I have already mentioned, you can also sell and run your online courses and programs on an online education platform like Teachable or Thinkific. These platforms will allow you to create and house your online programs on their site and they also provide an online store where you will sell your courses.

In-Person Events and Retreats

If you hold in-person events and retreats you will be selling them online, but of course you will be running them on location. I use Shopify to sell my retreat registrations as it offers easy product variations, and good tracking and reporting. But as I have mentioned you can also use an online ticket service like Eventbrite, Ticket Tailor or Brown Paper Ticket. I have used these kinds of services at different times and when your business is young this may be a good place to start. They are easy to use and although they will become too costly as your business grows, they offer a convenient way to start while your ticket volume is small. Once you have sold a ticket to your retreat or event an email will automatically be sent either from the email service your using, ie. MailChimp. or through a ticketing platform. The email will give people all the information they need to make their way to the retreat or event. I usually send a series of emails leading up to the start date with information about travel and details of what to bring and what to expect so that people feel well cared for and don't have anything to worry about.

YOU'VE KNOWN THIS MOMENT WAS COMIMG...

I hope you now see that building a business is not only possible, but also inherently fulfilling.

Some Final Words of Encouragement

So now it's time for a good ol' fashioned pep talk. You are an Artist of Possibility. You've devoted yourself for years, or maybe decades, in a search for the deeper meaning of human life - and you've found it, or at least part of it. You've discovered something that transformed your life and now you want to share it so that it can have the same miraculous effect on other people's lives. You want to devote yourself fulltime to sharing the wisdom and the insight you've gained, and the practices and techniques you've mastered. And you've decided that you want to set up an online business so that you can deliver what you have of value to the people who want it. I applaud you for your vision and your courage.

There will undoubtedly be some of you who are eager and ready to get started building your business. You've known this moment was coming and I hope that this book has helped show you that building a business is not only possible, but also inherently fulfilling. Others of you, no doubt, are more reluctant or intimidated at the prospect of building a business. I understand that. Building a business is not what you had in mind as you pursued deeper wisdom. I hope that for you this book has offered a vision of business that not only seems possible, but also attractive and perhaps even inspiring.

I hope that I have convinced you that building a business is not just a path to abundance, it can, and ultimately must be, a source of abundance right now. Building a business in the way that we have been speaking about it is a joy to do. That's because your passion is sharing your wisdom, and every step in the process of creating and maintaining your business is part of the process of sharing. When your business is based on communications and your communications are all sharing the wisdom you want to give, then the business is a source of abundance. Even when you are working on the business of your business, you are doing what you love, with people you love, for reasons you love.

I also recognize, and want to be sure that you recognize, that what you want to do is not just good for you. It is essential for the betterment of life on this planet. There was a reason you started searching for deeper wisdom in the first place. Part of it was personal, you wanted to be happy and fulfilled, but that probably wasn't all of it. If you are like me, you were also motivated because you knew that human life, and all life on this planet could be so much better. You saw the suffering in the world and you realized that a great deal of it at least was unnecessary.

Supposedly there is a Chinese curse that says, "*may you live in interesting times.*" The implication is that life is a lot easier when times are simple. Interesting times means challenging times. Well, if we look around I think most of us would agree that we live in interesting times. Our species faces mounting social, political and economic challenges of all kinds. Even the ecology of the planet that sustains our lives appears to be in peril. The future of life on this planet is far from guaranteed. We certainly live in interesting times.

Whatever it is that you have discovered and now want to devote your life to sharing is part of the antidote to the troubles of this world. It is almost certainly not the entire solution, but is a piece of what is needed. Maybe you offer programs that will help people live healthier and happier lives, or that will open their hearts and minds to a deeper perception of reality, or that will show them how to live in deeper harmony with all of life on this planet. Whatever it is, I am certain, it is part of what the world needs right now. That is why you are so excited to share it.

As I said in the first chapter of this book, we live in a world that often seems to be overwhelmed with the darkness that comes from a lack of awareness of the deeper potentials of the human spirit. While at the same time, many of us, probably largely outside of the public eye, have done profound inner work that has revealed depths of insight and understanding that our world desperately needs. You are one of those, you are part of a great untapped human resource. The wealth of wisdom that you have to offer is needed in the world. Your business will allow you to share it.

Congratulations on taking this step.

A COMMON ATTRIBUTE SHARED BY ALL <u>FAILED</u> BUSINESS PEOPLE IS

they give up trying.

A COMMON ATTRIBUTE SHARED BY ALL <u>SUCCESSFUL</u> BUSINESS PEOPLE IS

they dont give up.

Works Cited

Brophy, Maria. *Art Money Success: A complete and easy-to-follow system for the artist who wasn't born with a business mind.* San Clemente. Son of the Sea, Inc, 2017

Carreira, Jeff. *The Gift of Spiritual Abundance: Five Principles for Being Happy & Fulfilled Right Now.* Philadelphia, Emergence Education, 2020

Content Marketing Institute. Informa PLC, London. Contentmarketinginstitute.com

Gerber, Michael E. *The E-Myth Revisited: Why Most Small Businesses Don't Work and What to Do About It.* New York, HarperCollins, 2001

Truant, Johnny B. and Platt, Sean. *Write, Publish, Repeat: The No-Luck-Required Guide to Self-Publishing Success.* Austin, Sterling & Stone, 2014

About the Authors

FOR NEARLY TWO DECADES **Jeff Carreira** has taught meditation and mystical philosophy online and in retreats held around the world. He is the author of more than twenty-five books including: *The Art of Conscious Contentment, The Experience of Luminous Absorption, The Gift of Spiritual Abundance, The Soul of a New Self, American Awakening* and *Higher Self Expression*.

In addition to his work as a teacher and writer, Jeff spent 12 years as the marketing and education director of an organization that created and distributed online products to thousands of people throughout the world. He has also been a founding partner of three other online business ventures including Emergence Education, the publishing house and online education business that he currently operates.

For more information about Jeff visit JeffCarreira.com

Sophie Peirce has been a business partner with Jeff Carreira in Emergence Education for five years. She has created numerous websites for the promotion and distribution of online programs and products. She created and manages a sophisticated web-based membership platform and is instrumental in overseeing content production, course delivery, and member services. In addition Sophie participates in the visioning and ongoing creative development of the business.

Made in the USA
Las Vegas, NV
01 June 2022